How to Vanquish a Virus

The truth about viruses, vaccines, and more!

Dedicated to Akira and Kailani

Published in 2021 by Welbeck Children's Books Limited
An imprint of the Welbeck Publishing Group
20 Mortimer Street, London W1T 3JW

Text copyright © 2021 Paul Ian Cross
Published by arrangement with Speckled Pen Limited

Illustration © Welbeck Publishing Limited,
part of Welbeck Publishing Group

ISBN: 978 1 78312 731 3

Writer: Paul Ian Cross, PhD
Illustrator: Steve Brown
Designer: Luke Griffin
Design Manager: Matt Drew
Editorial Manager: Joff Brown
Production: Melanie Richardson

Printed in the UK
10 9 8 7 6 5 4 3 2 1

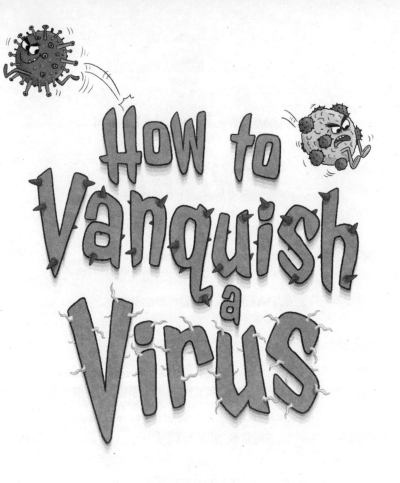

How to Vanquish a Virus

WELBECK

Paul Ian Cross, PhD

Illustrated by Steve Brown

CONTENTS

INTRODUCTION

There are more viruses on Planet Earth than there are stars in the universe! But why should we care about germs that are smaller than a pin head?

BECAUSE THEY ARE OUR FUTURE!
Every new virus (and lots of old ones) allows scientists to learn fascinating facts to help us come up with new medicines and inventions.

BECAUSE THEY ARE STRONG!
A virus can change shape, it can steal, it can bring in reinforcements. Think of a virus as a zombie! Scientists need to be clever, quick, and creative.

BECAUSE VIRUSES MAKE US BETTER HUMAN BEINGS!
If you want to vanquish a virus, this is the book for you.
We'll explore the top viruses in history, and show
how to create a new medicine in super-fast time.
By the time you finish reading this book you will be:

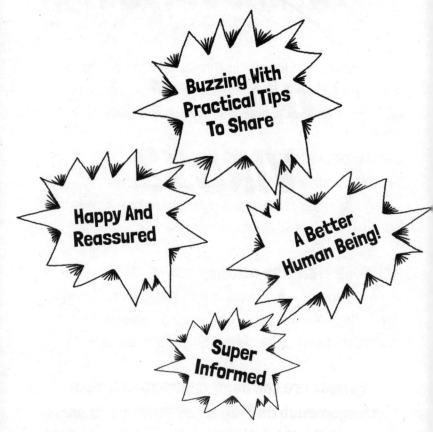

Buzzing With Practical Tips To Share

Happy And Reassured

A Better Human Being!

Super Informed

Ready?
Then let's dive into the fascinating world of viruses.

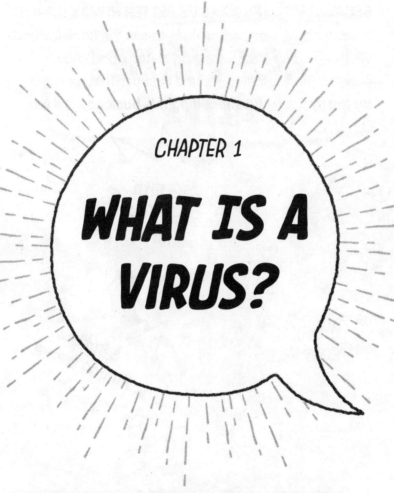

CHAPTER 1

WHAT IS A VIRUS?

Viruses are the most common biological thingamabob on Planet Earth. Some clever science folks think that if you stacked up all the viruses on earth, they could reach from one side of the Milky Way to the other.

ARE VIRUSES ALIVE?

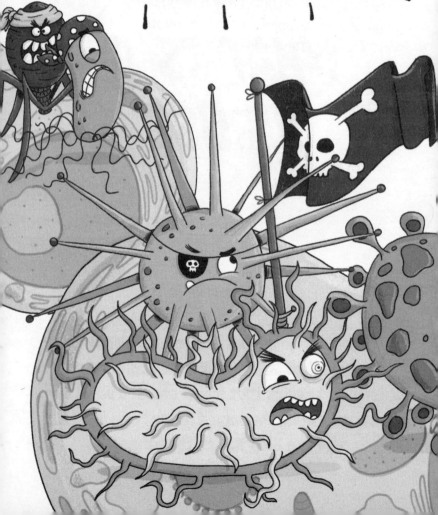

Viruses are not classed as living things and they're not quite organisms either. But scientists agree that they are strange—perhaps on the edge of life. Weird! Think of them as zombie-like pirate-vampires.

Viruses need other organisms to survive and reproduce, because they're not able to make energy themselves. They can't function outside of a living cell, which is why they are seen as zombies—I mean pirates. Or maybe both! Ahoy, Me Bities!

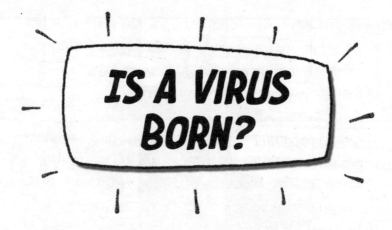

IS A VIRUS BORN?

The "life" of a virus all starts with a single viral particle called a virion. Lots of virions make up a virus. The virion can "survive" outside a cell for a while, but it won't activate until it's inside.

Once a virion comes into contact with a cell, it clamps onto the surface and checks to see if it has matching protein keys. If there's a fit, the virus is able to unlock the door to the cell and get inside!

Different viruses have different keys. They can only get into cells with the correct type of key.

Once inside, the virus is like a little microscopic molecular machine that cause chaos inside the cell, hijacking it. Like pirates taking over a ship!

Inside the cell, the virus manages to reprogram the cell to produce more viruses. The cell becomes a virus-making factory! So many viruses are produced that the cell swells and bursts like a sack of slime! Yuck! Then it kills the poor cell!

The virus floods outside, and the whole process starts again. Virions land on the surface of nearby cells, infecting them. As the infection spreads, the virus becomes more powerful. Watch out—the virus is taking over!

11

WHAT ARE VIRUSES MADE OF?

Viruses are basically a blob of genetic material surrounded by a protein coat. The genetic material—called the genome—sits in the middle of the virion. The genome is made up of a molecule of Deoxyribonucleic Acid (DNA) or Ribonucleic Acid (RNA). These molecules are types of nucleic acid.

They're basically a set of instructions, like a recipe, showing how to make more virus. The main function of a viral genome is to store the instructions for building more virus particles. The genome is wrapped up in a protein coat called a capsid, keeping the genome nice and safe inside. Some viruses, but not all, have an extra later of fatty molecules, called lipids, around them.

The extra layer is called an envelope. Not like the envelope you post your Nan's birthday card in! **No!** The coronavirus that causes COVID-19 is like this. It is an "enveloped" virus.

HAPPY BIRTHDAY

Did you know that soap can dissolve this fatty envelope, leading to the destruction of the whole virion? That's why washing your hands with soap is so important!

ARE VIRUSES AND BACTERIA THE SAME?

No! Viruses and bacteria are both types of "microorganism" but they're very different. When it comes to size, bacteria win this prize. Viruses are super small in comparison.

Bacteria are single-celled organisms. This means they have a cell wall. Viruses don't have a cell wall, so they are literally squishy bags of genetic material!

They also exist in very different ways. Bacteria are free-living and can live inside or outside a person or animal, while viruses are unable to reproduce without someone—or something—else.

Viruses infect cells, which means ... yes! You guessed it: some viruses even infect bacteria! These types of viruses are called Bacteriophages. They look a bit like the moon landers from the 1960s!

THE ROGUES' GALLERY OF VIRUSES

6500 NM
6000 NM
5500 NM
5000 NM
4500 NM
4000 NM
3500 NM
3000 NM
2500 NM

VANQUISH POLICE DEPT
PHAGE
12461
CRIME: VIRUS

VANQUISH POLICE DEPT
EBOLA
21814
CRIME: VIRUS

VANQUISH POLICE DEPT
MERS
18943
CRIME: VIRUS

Viruses come in many shapes and sizes. They're so small you'll need an electron microscope to see them—they're super tiny. That's why they're hard to contain if there is an outbreak, because they're invisible to the naked eye.

Many coronaviruses are spherical in shape, while Ebola is long and stringy. Bacteriophages, the moon lander wannabes, are the smallest.

VANQUISH POLICE DEPT
SARS
99132
CRIME:**VIRUS**

VANQUISH POLICE DEPT
HIV
13341
CRIME:**VIRUS**

THE PERFECT HOST

When a virus gets inside you, you become something called a host. Hosts can be people, animals, plants, and even bacteria!

Remember, it's not just viruses that can make you ill. Sometimes illness is caused by bacteria. Some bacteria can cause food poisoning and others can infect cuts and wounds. Ouch! Other illnesses can be caused by parasites too—like the parasite that gives you Malaria. That parasite is called Plasmodium.

Different infections need different medicines to treat them. But we should remember that not all bacteria and viruses are bad. Many live in harmony with us. While most types of virus are harmless to humans, some can make you very sick. And some can even be deadly...

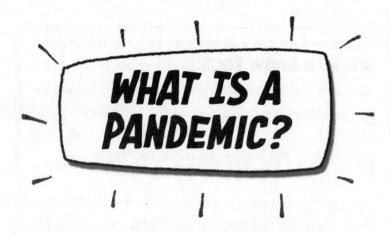

WHAT IS A PANDEMIC?

When a virus spreads from person to person, there's a chance it will keep on going. If a virus spreads within a community of people, it is known as an "epidemic." The word comes from Ancient Greek: "epi" is the Ancient Greek word for "upon", and "demos" means "people."

This may be followed by something bigger—and more far-reaching. The Ancient Greek word for "all" is "pan." When you put "pan" with "people" (demos), you get "pandemic." So a pandemic is an illness that spreads all around the world.

Need to know facts:

☼ A virus is a tiny germ.

☼ They're so small you can't see them!

☼ Viruses are not quite organisms
   or living things. They're
   zombie-like pirate vampires!

☼ They can float through the air
   and in tiny drops of water.

☼ They can land and sit on surfaces.

☼ An epidemic is when a virus spreads in
   a local area, and a pandemic is when it
   spreads around the world.

Draw your own imaginary virus!

Check out the pictures of the different types of virus and make up your own. Why don't you dress it up in a spiky coat or put a slimy DNA viral code inside?

Use your imagination and make up something super gross!

CHAPTER 2

CRAFTY
COVID-19

Coronavirus is a virus that has spread
around the world. The virus causes an
illness called COVID–19.

WHAT ARE CORONAVIRUSES?

You've heard a lot about coronaviruses, and you've DEFINITELY heard about one of them. They're a group of viruses from the viral family *coronaviridae*. They have a simple structure:

⚙ **SPHERICAL**
⚙ **COATED WITH SPIKES OF PROTEIN**

These spikes help the virus attach to human cells, in order to infect them.

Coronaviruses get their name from the way they look. When viewed under a powerful electron microscope, they look like they're wearing a crown. Like the Queen of England, but with less diamonds! They also look like how the sun appears during a solar eclipse!

- "Corona" is the Latin word for "crown".
- The sun's corona is the outer layer of its atmosphere.

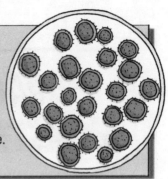

There are currently seven coronaviruses known to infect humans, causing different illnesses.

Human Coronavirus Name	Illness
HCoV–NL63	Types of common cold
HCoV–229E	
HCoV–OC43	
HKU1	
SARS–CoV	Severe acute respiratory syndrome (SARS)
MERS–CoV	Middle East respiratory syndrome (MERS)
SARS–CoV–2	COVID–19

Fortunately, most coronaviruses are not too serious, such as those that cause common colds. But some can be a lot more dangerous …

SAVAGE SARS, MONSTROUS MERS

In 2002, a type of coronavirus began to infect people in Asia. The virus was named SARS-CoV and caused something called Severe Acute Respiratory Syndrome or SARS—a serious breathing disease.

In 2012, another type of coronavirus appeared, this time in the Middle East. This one caused a disease called Middle East Respiratory Syndrome or MERS. SARS and MERS went on to affect many countries. Fortunately, both epidemics were limited and contained. Phew!

But scientists around the world were worried that another type of coronavirus could one day cause a global PANDEMIC. We'd been relatively lucky with SARS, then again with MERS. Would we be so lucky a third time? We were not.

One research team in Oxford, led by Professor Sarah Gilbert, developed a vaccine for MERS for this very reason. What if another virus comes along? Sarah's research would end up having far-reaching consequences, preparing us for a virus that would change the world.

Where in the World?

Where SARS, MERS and COVID-19 were first identified.

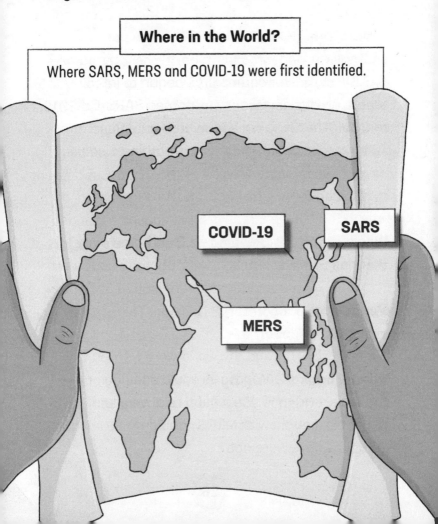

SARS-COV-2

In the winter of 2019, a brand-new type of coronavirus appeared in China. It was later named SARS-CoV-2. This virus causes another serious breathing disease called Coronavirus Disease 2019, or COVID-19 for short. You've probably heard of it! This virus has changed the world in ways we could never have imagined—some of them bad, but a few of them good too.

Where did SARS-CoV-2 come from? There are lots of theories ...

Maybe from a laboratory? Unlikely. There is no evidence to support this.

Natural origins ... Yes! By looking at the genome of the virus, evidence suggests that it jumped from bats to people, or via another animal first.

But where did the virus REALLY come from?
Honestly, we'll probably never know the exact details.
But most viruses come from sources that no one
can trace back ... and a lot of them have still been
overcome.

The most important thing we can do is to find new
treatments to reduce the virus's effects and create
vaccines to reduce the likelihood of people passing
the virus on.

HOW DOES COVID-19 WORK?

Some people say this disease works in the same way as influenza—the flu.

THOSE PEOPLE ARE WRONG!

For most of us, the flu is a mild disease with no long-term effects. However, SARS-CoV-2 does have other effects and it may cause long term symptoms and illnesses. This is the reason the world had to go into lockdown, to limit the spread and protect people from infection.

A serious effect of SARS-CoV-2 is that it reduces the lung's ability to transfer oxygen from the air into our blood. This leads to low blood oxygen levels. This is called hypoxia. Many people with this problem need to be admitted to the hospital.

The disease becomes serious if the virus enters the lungs and multiplies. This directly damages the lung cells and may lead to pneumonia (fluid in the lungs).

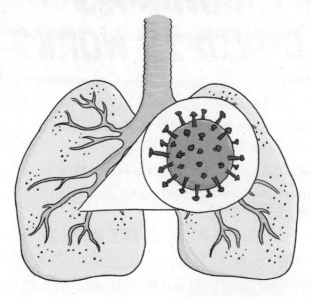

The older you are, the more serious the disease can be.

Over time, we have discovered that SARS-CoV-2 infects many types of cells, not just the lungs. Some people also continue to report symptoms many months after they were originally infected. This has been given the name **LONG COVID**.

This can be scary, but the good news is the WHOLE WORLD continues to work together to find medicines and vaccines!

THE INFODEMIC

It's not just COVID-19 we need to worry about. It's the misinformation surrounding COVID-19 too!

There's the pandemic, and then there's the infodemic—a new word made to describe the spread of false information!

Whether it's a terrific tweet or a tantalizing TikTok, sometimes going viral is a good thing. But now, something else has been going viral and it is changing the world in really bad ways.

Do you know what it is?
It's misinformation!

Misinformation is when someone shares something incorrect by accident. That means they didn't know what they were sharing was wrong. But there's something even worse. It's called **disinformation**! That's when someone does it on purpose!

Sometimes people or groups share fake news or false information that is either wrong or untested, and since the COVID-19 pandemic, it's worse than ever!

It's very important to follow advice from trusted sources, but this is not always easy! What happens when the wrong information gets shared? It can have a bad effect on people's health, as they may follow information that's wrong for them.

DIGITAL DETECTIVES

Your mission, if you choose to accept it, is to become a DIGITAL DETECTIVE. We all have a responsibility to learn, understand, and share real and accurate information. We may not always get things right, but as long as we learn from mistakes and try to improve, we'll end up with a happier and healthier society!

Did You Know?

Nearly 60% of "facts" shared on digital platforms can be false! This is why we need you to become a digital detective.

Here are six handy rules to beat misinformation!

1. Always try to follow advice from trustworthy sources—like your local doctor, or the World Health Organisation (WHO).

2. Read beyond the headline—do you believe ALL the details behind the most obvious ones?

3. Analyze information. This means checking the facts. You can do this by going to at least two other sources of the same story!

4. If someone tells you something that sounds impossible, ask how they got the information. Don't believe everything just because your best friend said it!

5. If you spot spelling mistakes in a piece of writing, it may not be a checked source.

6. Just because someone is famous, it doesn't make them an expert! Even celebrities get things wrong.

We can defeat misinformation together—as long as we all become digital detectives!

Design a Face Covering

SARS-CoV-2 mostly spreads through the air and sometimes hangs about on surfaces. So one of the best ways to help stop the spread of the disease is with facemasks. If you could have anything on your face covering, what would it be? Your favorite cartoon character? Favorite animal? A unicorn? (Mine would totally be a unicorn.) Or what about a T. REX?

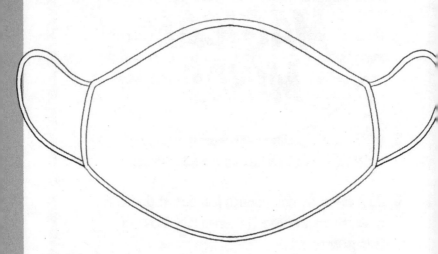

Copy the template onto a large piece of paper, and design a cool new mask. Now get a kids' disposable facemask and draw your design on it. (Ask your parents for a mask first!)

CHAPTER 3

BATTLING BODIES, MAGICAL MINDS

Many of us struggled to maintain our mental and physical health during the coronavirus (COVID-19) pandemic. This section helps you understand how to support yourself.

BRILLIANT BODIES!

The human body is an incredible metropolis of trillions of cells. Together, these cells make terrific tissues. Lots of tissues make awesome organs. Lots of awesome organs make brilliant body systems, and brilliant body systems make ...

A HUMAN!

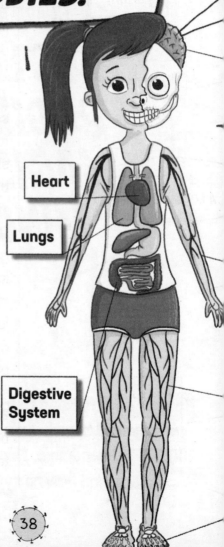

Heart

Lungs

Digestive System

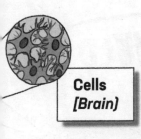

Cells [Brain]

Brain

I'VE GOT A LOT GOING ON!

Circulatory System

Nervous System

Skeleton

Cells—there are about 37 trillion cells in the average human body! Different types of cell undertake different jobs, like carrying oxygen or destroying invaders.

Tissues—cells doing the same job are grouped together as tissues, like skin, muscle and even blood.

Organs—different tissues group together into larger structures called organs. Your brain, heart, lungs, liver, and kidneys are all examples of organs.

Body Systems—each body system has a job to do.

HOW TO BUILD A HUMAN

Cells are the body's building blocks, and there are more than two hundred different types—each with different jobs. Cells are constantly dividing. They do this so that the body can grow or repair itself.

When a cell splits, it becomes two new cells. These are called daughter cells. The process is called mitosis.

Every cell has a nucleus—this is its control center. The nucleus of every human cell carries something very important inside. Buried treasure? No. A map to buried treasure? No, but almost. Each nucleus holds a unique blueprint—sort of like a map! This blueprint of genetic material is called Deoxyribonucleic Acid—or DNA for short. DNA is a "nucleic acid".

DNA is bundled into chromosomes. Each chromosome contains all the information needed to build and maintain a human being. You could call it a recipe for life.

A RECIPE FOR LIFE

DNA is shaped like a twisted ladder, called a double helix. The rungs of the ladder contain different combinations of chemical units called bases. Each section of the ladder is known as a gene—a unique sequence. Our genes contain our unique blueprint—our recipe for life.

Genes tell our cells how to make things a certain way. They code for someone's unique characteristics, such as a person's eye color or how tall they are.

But at the heart of all this, our DNA is needed to make proteins. DNA needs help to do this, and uses something called messenger RNA (mRNA). Proteins are VERY important in the human body! Our individual recipe for life makes us all totally unique!

DESIGNED TO DEFEND

The human body is a FORTRESS, built to defend against pathogens. A pathogen is the name given to anything bad that wants to invade a body—such as bacteria, viruses, parasites, or fungi.

Remember, when it comes to bacteria—not all are bad. We need many types of bacteria in our tummies to have great gut health! These friendly bacteria would not be classed as pathogens. Pathogens are the bad ones.

A pathogen will fight hard to get inside. Like a Minecraft mob, but WAY COOLER. And SCARIER!

Fortunately for you and I, our BRILLIANT BODIES have some BRILLIANT BARRIERS to slow these rascals down.

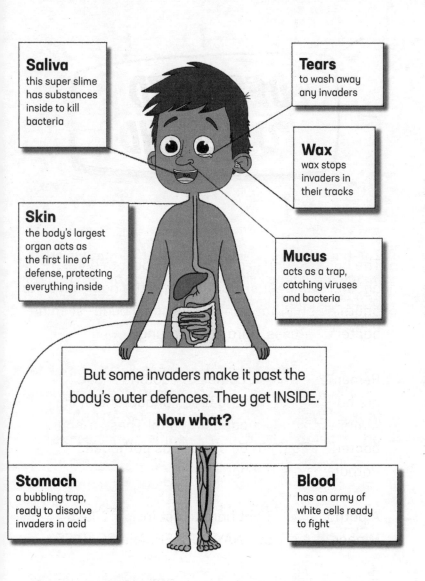

Saliva
this super slime has substances inside to kill bacteria

Tears
to wash away any invaders

Wax
wax stops invaders in their tracks

Skin
the body's largest organ acts as the first line of defense, protecting everything inside

Mucus
acts as a trap, catching viruses and bacteria

But some invaders make it past the body's outer defences. They get INSIDE.
Now what?

Stomach
a bubbling trap, ready to dissolve invaders in acid

Blood
has an army of white cells ready to fight

If the invaders get past all of that, it's time to activate the incredible IMMUNE SYSTEM!

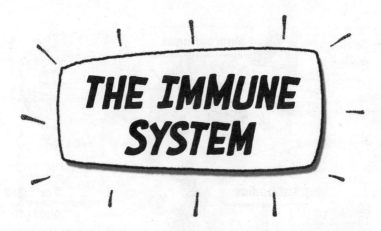

THE IMMUNE SYSTEM

The body's defenses are known as the immune system. Imagine them as killer robots with zap guns. They track and target pathogens once they're inside a body and... ZAP!

The body needs to identify pathogens, so that it knows exactly what to zap and when. How does it know what to zap? Well, by recognizing antigens. An antigen is any substance that causes your immune system to respond—for example, a protein on the outside of a virus or bacteria. Over time, the body remembers the pathogens, so it can get rid of them quicker the next time they attack.

The body does all this by producing special trackers called antibodies. These are proteins that attach themselves to the invaders, alerting the body's systems to ... DESTROY!

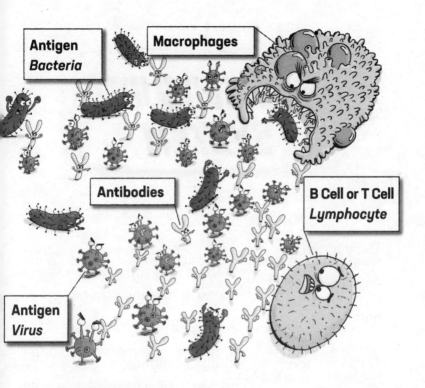

Labels within illustration: **Antigen** *Bacteria*, **Macrophages**, **Antibodies**, **B Cell or T Cell** *Lymphocyte*, **Antigen** *Virus*

AWESOME ANTIBODIES

When the body recognizes an invader, the body releases a flood of antibodies to attach to the outer surface of the pathogen.

But what else can help?

WHITE BLOOD CELLS!

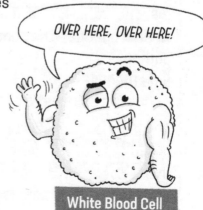

OVER HERE, OVER HERE!

White Blood Cell

SOLDIERS FOR VICTORY!

There's an army waiting ... and they're ready to fight!
These are white blood cells.

Even if the pathogen evades all other defenses,
antibodies can still attach to it—and there's only one
way this is going to end.

White Blood Cells

☼ **Macrophage**—they engulf bacteria and eat them

☼ **Lymphocyte**—they help to release antibodies,
helping locate the invaders for their comrades

☼ **Neutrophil**—the most common type, they
attack bacteria and fungi

Once antibodies flood over an invader, the body starts a destruction of the infected cells. This allows the body to clear itself of both the invaders and the damaged cells.

And this means...

VICTORY!

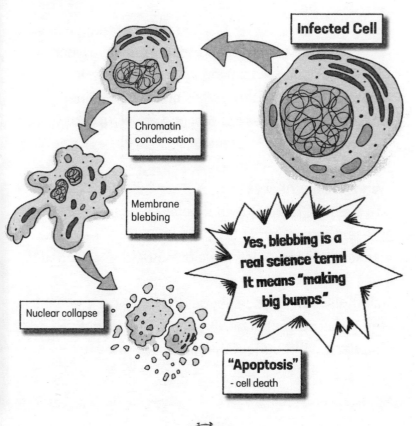

Infected Cell

Chromatin condensation

Membrane blebbing

Yes, blebbing is a real science term! It means "making big bumps."

Nuclear collapse

"Apoptosis" - cell death

MAGICAL MINDS

Mental health is really important, especially when we're physically ill. Looking after our mind will help our overall health. This is called mindfulness. Mindfulness reduces our feelings of worry, and increases joy and happiness.

What is mindfulness?

It's a simple technique that helps us focus on the present moment—not the past or future. If we center ourselves in the present, we can stop these worries.

Mindfulness brings us peace and helps us to accept things we can't change, like scary things that are happening throughout the world.

One way of practicing mindfulness is through **meditation**. This practice originated in ancient India, and has a long history in Hinduism.

A MINUTE OF MINDFULNESS

- ☼ Close your eyes.
- ☼ Take a deep breath.
- ☼ Listen to the sounds around you.
- ☼ Imagine you're beside a flowing river.
- ☼ You can hear the water rushing over the rocks.
- ☼ Open your eyes.
- ☼ How do you feel now?

GREAT!

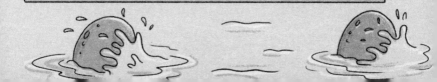

Green Fingers!

The outdoors can help you relax and connect with Planet Earth. You can look at the buds on trees or take part in a butterfly count. Even better, you can help some nature sprout! You could tend to a yard or windowsill. Plant some wildflower seeds and just watch what happens.

WHAT TO DO:

1. Find a spot in your yard or put a window box out.

2. Scatter some compost. Compost is just like the human body—it helps things grow!

WHAT YOU'LL NEED:
Flower Seeds
A Plant Pot
Water
Compost

3. Now, mix your seeds and spread them over the compost.

4. Add a thin layer of more compost and sprinkle some water.

5. Keep watering ... and watering. Not too much—just enough so that the seeds drink it all up.

6. In a few weeks, you'll see some seedlings. All thanks to you! All they need to grow is water and sunshine.

Congratulations! You are now a happy gardener.

CHAPTER 4

SUPER SCIENTISTS

Is it a bird? NO.
Is it a plane? NO!
It's a group of very excited
SUPER SCIENTISTS!

WHAT DOES A SCIENTIST DO?

All sorts of people are involved in vanquishing a virus—from key workers to shop staff to the person in the street. We can all help conquer a virus or any other disease. (There are rumors that even scientists have been involved!)

But what exactly does a scientist look like and what do they DO?

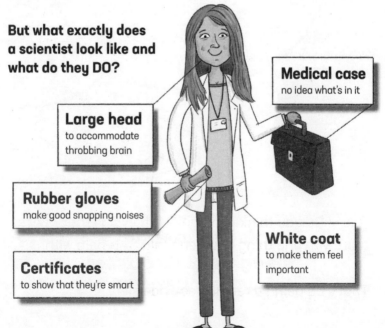

Medical case
no idea what's in it

Large head
to accommodate throbbing brain

Rubber gloves
make good snapping noises

White coat
to make them feel important

Certificates
to show that they're smart

OK, maybe it's not quite like that...

Scientists are our superheroes who possess all sorts of medical know-how. Here are a few things they do:

Phew! Do you think you could achieve all that? Let's start with one thing you definitely CAN help with.

That's by being a real-life science sleuth!

SCIENCE SLEUTHS

Some scientists specialize in Health Research. This is really important when we are dealing with a virus. Scientists around the world work together without arguing—not even over who got the best birthday presents!

CORONAVIRUS DOES NOT RESPECT BORDERS, AND THE IMPACT OF THE PANDEMIC IS BEING FELT ACROSS THE GLOBE.

Dr. Lesong Conteh

Start your own sleuthing by finding the following key words in this Science Word Square. These words describe the important actions Health Researchers take. There are two hidden words that scientists definitely do NOT use. Can you guess which they are?

V	E	J	H	S	H	Q	S	Y	F	U	L	V	V	T
H	C	P	A	I	G	R	U	K	N	Q	Y	T	E	O
W	U	W	Y	H	T	X	B	D	C	D	T	C	G	N
M	D	Z	R	D	E	V	E	L	O	P	N	A	A	Q
J	E	U	A	G	S	R	E	Y	R	K	E	H	M	T
V	R	A	U	J	S	R	E	X	A	T	L	D	A	O
N	J	P	R	T	U	R	N	P	P	K	X	J	D	S
Q	J	N	A	S	V	Z	R	T	P	F	E	M	F	G
A	D	N	A	V	F	H	A	W	R	I	X	R	B	W
W	D	E	N	W	F	M	P	J	E	Y	P	V	C	H
K	M	C	U	I	M	P	R	O	V	E	L	G	N	O
G	U	D	K	C	O	Q	V	C	E	R	O	F	Z	X
E	D	J	D	B	G	C	B	N	N	I	R	T	H	N
C	O	N	F	U	S	E	W	J	T	D	E	P	Q	L

Find all these words ... plus two scientists don't use!

Develop
new vaccines

Understand
mental health issues

Prevent
the spread of a virus

Measure
how long a patient stays immune

Reduce
malnutrition and pollution

Explore
the impact of a virus on health services

Partner
The UK, Brazil, and South Africa worked together to test a vaccine for COVID-19

Improve
gaps in knowledge

HIDDEN WORDS: Damage, Confuse

57

SHAPING SCIENCE

Anyone can help shape science—even you! Here are some examples of Super Scientists who didn't realize they were about to change the world.

Louis Pasteur was a 19th-century French chemist, until he discovered the importance of... washing hands. He realized that germs could be carried on skin. Soap became a superhero!

Ryan White

Ryan White was a teenager from Indiana, USA who helped doctors understand that HIV could affect anyone. He had hemophilia, which is a bleeding disorder. This condition meant that he needed blood transfusions. But the blood he received was infected with HIV, and he became infected. Ryan bravely made a big difference to our understanding of how HIV can be transmitted.

Lois Gibbs lived in New York and couldn't understand why her two children kept falling ill. She discovered huge amounts of toxic waste in her neighborhood. This helped us all understand how important it is to recycle waste in a careful way. She went on to become an environmental activist.

Lois Gibbs

COOL CAREERS

There are many different types of scientists. Scientists who study space are called astronomers. Those that study rocks are geologists. Nature? They're called biologists. Scientists who study microbes are microbiologists.

But not all scientists are the same.

Dr. Raven Baxter is a molecular biologist and science communicator ... who is also a rapper and makes music about science. Scientists can be VERY creative!

But despite all their different interests, when a pandemic comes along, scientists work together. One group who are vital during a pandemic are ... virologists.

They study viruses to learn how they transmit and infect us—and also how viruses mutate, or change.

COMMUNITY HEALTH

All of these people are involved in vanquishing a virus! It's how we work together that counts.

The front line is the most difficult place to work during a pandemic. The front line refers to doctors, nurses, and other people who look after patients with COVID-19 in hospitals.

Dr. Kai Lee
hospital doctor

Some front line are people called clinical staff. They help people in the hospital to survive many different viruses, including COVID-19.

Some of these staff are super interested in lungs, and how a virus affects them...

Tracey Van Wyk
hospital improver

Emma Lee
research nurse

Did You Know?

○ A normal adult lung is 9.5 inches in height—taller than a water bottle!

○ The left lung is narrower because it has to make room for the heart, which is the size of a fist.

○ If you have asthma, you need to be extra careful around illnesses such as COVID-19.

○ Older people have lung tissues that are less elastic, which is one of the reasons why they are more vulnerable to illness.

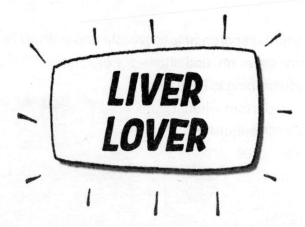

LIVER LOVER

Dr. Zania Stamataki from Birmingham, England has researched the liver for most of her career. Here are some of the fascinating facts she has to share with you:

☼ **Your liver is 96% water**

☼ **It's bigger than your brain!**

☼ **A liver can rebuild itself from scratch**

☼ **It has over 500 functions**

But what do livers have to do with viruses? Well, Dr. Stamataki looked into how SARS-CoV-2 enters our bodies by the nose, mouth, or eyes and also how it moves between people. Once inside, a virus can affect different organs, including the liver.

Zania's research helped people understand transmission, and showed that social distancing is REALLY important when it comes to vanquishing THIS virus.

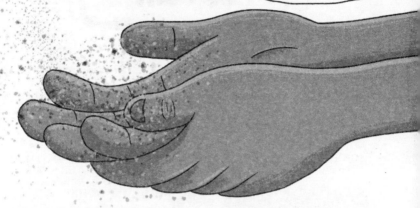

GLIMMER, SHIMMER, GERMS ON MY DINNER!

SEE HOW GERMS SPREAD!

☼ Put a tiny sprinkle of glitter on your friends' hands.

☼ Make sure you use biodegradable glitter to help keep our environment safe.

☼ Now wash your hands and try and get rid of it. How much glitter is left in the sink?

☼ Viruses and bacteria have a way of clinging on just like the glitter does, so it's super important we wash our hands properly.

MAPPING MEDICINE

Science knows no borders—anyone, anywhere at any time can help. Across history and around the world, people have worked hard to conquer viruses. Some of these people are hardly remembered—like Mary Hunt, known as 'Moldy Mary', the woman who found penicillin from a moldy cantaloupe in 1943. But others made their mark.

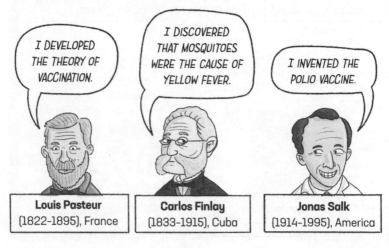

I DEVELOPED THE THEORY OF VACCINATION.

Louis Pasteur
(1822–1895), France

I DISCOVERED THAT MOSQUITOES WERE THE CAUSE OF YELLOW FEVER.

Carlos Finlay
(1833–1915), Cuba

I INVENTED THE POLIO VACCINE.

Jonas Salk
(1914–1995), America

I WAS FIRST TO SPOT CORONOVIRUS WITH AN ELECTRON MICROSCOPE.

June Almeida
(1930-2007), Scotland

I IDENTIFIED THE RETROVIRUS CALLED HIV.

Luc Montagnier
(1932–), France

I CREATED THE SMALLPOX VACCINE.

Edward Jenner
(1749-1823), England

I DECLARED SMALLPOX OVER IN 1980.

Frank Fenner
(1914-2010), Australia

I WORKED ON DNA VACCINES.

Harriet Robinson,
USA

I DISCOVERED THAT HIV CAME FROM NONHUMAN PRIMATES.

Beatrice Hahn
(1955–), Germany/USA

I PROVED THAT CORONAVIRUS COMES FROM FRUIT-EATING BATS.

Shi Zhengli
(1964–), China

Grow Your Own Germs

Just like Moldy Mary, you can inspect your own mold!

WHAT TO DO:

1. Place a slice of bread in each bag.
2. Add water to one bag and place it in a dark place, like the bottom of your wardrobe.

> **WHAT YOU'LL NEED:**
> Three slices of bread
> Water
> Recyclable plastic bags

3. Put the other bagged bread in a sunny place, like a windowsill.
4. Shove the third piece of bread in the fridge!
5. Leave them all for a week. You can check in regularly to monitor growth!
6. Go back at the end of the week and record your results.

CONCLUSIONS:

Here are some hints to decide what you've discovered:

• Use a line graph to record mold growth.

• What does this show you about their conditions?

• Does light or heat make a difference?

Congratulations! You are now an expert in mold, the source of penicillin. Which makes you ... a Super Scientist.

CHAPTER 5

REMARKABLE RESEARCH

In an unprecedented race against time, the world worked together to learn how to vanquish the coronavirus. It was all done with some remarkable research!

MILKMAIDS MAKE MEDICINE!

In the 18th century, a boy named Edward Jenner explored the countryside. This led to an interest in how plants and animals could help us. He grew up to become a doctor—just like you could!

One of his early papers was on cuckoos, but his greatest achievement was learning how to prevent a disease called smallpox. He learned this by studying ... cowpox!

DID YOU KNOW THAT THE LATIN WORD "VACCA" MEANS 'COW'? THIS IS HOW WE GOT THE WORD "VACCINATION!"

Virologist Veronica

In 1796, Jenner heard about a milkmaid named Sarah with perfect skin, free of smallpox scars. She claimed that after catching cowpox from her favorite cow, Matilda*, she couldn't catch smallpox.

Jenner decided to explore the milkmaid's theory. He extracted protein-rich pus from a cowpox bubble on someone's flesh. (Ugh!) He then used this pus to create a substance called an inoculum.

After giving the inoculum to his gardener's 8-year-old son, James Phipps, James went on to develop a mild fever. A few weeks later, Jenner gave the boy another inoculum but this time it wasn't cowpox ... it was **SMALLPOX!**

But ... **SURPRISE!** James didn't get ill.

Jenner had found a way of preventing smallpox and he'd invented...

A VACCINE!

*Sources who knew the cow say she might have been called Blossom.

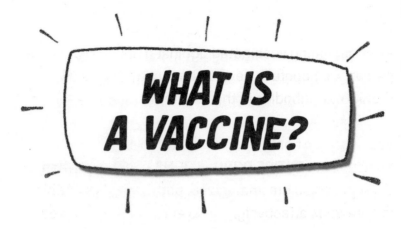

WHAT IS A VACCINE?

A vaccine works by teaching the body's immune system to recognize and destroy invaders.

By introducing a small amount of the pathogen into a person's system, the body can then be prepared. This means that the body's immune system can be ready to pounce on an invader.

After becoming vaccinated against a disease, a person will hopefully develop immunity. This is all thanks to antibodies in their system.

Vaccines don't only work for individuals. They protect **ENTIRE POPULATIONS** of people. When enough people are immunized, pathogens are unable to spread as effectively, and eventually they run out of people to infect!

This is why vaccines are so powerful. Unlike most medicines, which treat or cure diseases, vaccines prevent them.

RACING RESEARCH

When COVID-19 first popped into existence in 2020, there was a race against time. Doctors and nurses wanted to help ill patients SURVIVE the disease. At the time, there was no known cure.

But at the same time, other scientists were busy as bees on another very important job. They were determined to discover a vaccine.

The world of science went into overdrive! Not a panic, but it started moving at top speed to research the disease.

This began with:

- ⚙ **observing patients**
- ⚙ **learning how to treat them**
- ⚙ **testing different medicines**

Hundreds of research studies were created in different places around the world. Some of these included...

Scientists in the United States used Artificial Intelligence and computer models of the coronavirus to understand how drugs and vaccines could be improved.

The UK, Brazil, and South Africa tested a new vaccine together–with almost 12,000 volunteers taking part. In Cardiff, Wales, doctors took samples from thousands of people to check for tiny differences in the virus's genetic code. This helped us understand how the virus spread. Changes in the virus allow us to understand how it spread around the world.

EYES AND HANDS

When scientists want to understand a human's health, they have to use two important parts of their bodies:

EYES!
Scientists observe patients all the time, and make decisions based on what they see. Think about how you might watch a dance on TikTok and then try it in your kitchen!

HANDS!
Other times, scientists might gather groups of people to see what happens when medicine is prescribed to them. This is called a clinical trial. One group might be handed out medicine that the scientists already understand. The second group might be given a brand-new medicine.

Think about your own hands. You could give red fruit to one friend, and green fruit to another friend. Who likes what, best?

Clinical trials of medicines and vaccines are important because scientists need to show that the medicine or vaccine is safe and is proved to work.

Clinical Trial Phases

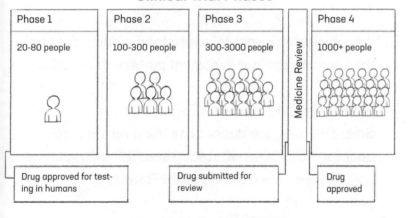

Phase 1	Phase 2	Phase 3	Medicine Review	Phase 4
20-80 people	100-300 people	300-3000 people		1000+ people

Drug approved for testing in humans

Drug submitted for review

Drug approved

Steroid Success

The award-shortlisted RECOVERY trial was a clinical trial based in the UK. It compared how different types of medicines worked for people suffering from COVID-19. One of the discoveries was that dexamethasone—a cheap steroid—could reduce the number of deaths by over a third!

VALIANT VOLUNTEERS

It wouldn't be possible to develop new medicines without the thousands of people who volunteer to take part in research!

These people are called study participants. They can be ANYONE! Healthy people or people with medical conditions. Moms, dads, brothers, sisters, grandmothers, grandfathers, children, and even—BABIES!

But—they all must CONSENT first. Consent means to give permission. As babies are too young to agree, someone has to say yes for them (normally Mom, Dad, or their guardian). There are lots of rules in place to protect people who take part in research.

Caring And Sharing

Dr. Shamaila Anwar has an important research job - she looks at why people from different communities hesitate about being involved in health research. Some don't want to take part in research. Others hesitate about taking new medicines. She's discovered that there are many reasons why people feel this way, and that it's important that scientists and doctors understand people's concerns. This is super-important for scientists. After all, just because scientists understand science, it doesn't mean that we all do!

Would YOU take part in a study if you were asked?

AMAZING VACCINE TECHNOLOGY

Some viruses like chickenpox and smallpox are made of DNA. Others are made of RNA—another molecule that can hold lots of information (see page 12).

RNA viruses have small genomes which regularly change. Protein spikes enable the immune system to see a virus. Bits of the spike can be used in vaccines to prompt the body to produce antibodies.

The first vaccines to be approved around the world involved two different technologies, which both used the SARS-CoV-2 spike protein to generate an immune response.

mRNA vaccine—a tiny piece of RNA is delivered to the cell inside a drop of fat called a lipid. It's just like delivering a letter! The cell reads the letter, learns how to make the spike protein, and then shreds the letter!

Modified viral vector vaccine—the genetic material is carried inside a modified chimpanzee virus. It's just like a TROJAN HORSE! The body learns how to fight the coronavirus from the information provided, generating an immune response! Clever. And SNEAKY too! No chimpanzees were harmed. But quite a few chimpanzee viruses were.

RESEARCH IS CREATING NEW KNOWLEDGE.

Neil Armstrong, astronaut

Activity Time

Invent a New Medicine

If you were a medical miracle worker, what type of medicine would you make?

Draw a design for your medicine. What name would you give it?

FOR EXAMPLE, YOU MIGHT MAKE:
tablets
an inhaler
an injection (ouch!)
syrup
lotion
patches

Draw your medicine here or on a separate piece of paper!

CHAPTER 6

HISTORY GOES VIRAL

Viruses might sound terribly modern.
But they've been around for the whole
of human history – we just didn't
always know what they were...

Which of these facts are true?

⚙ The word "virus" was used by the Romans to mean poison. TRUE/FALSE

⚙ Yellow Fever was the first "human" virus to be found in 1881. TRUE/FALSE

⚙ It wasn't until the electron microscope was invented in 1931 that we could actually see viruses. TRUE/FALSE

⚙ The woman who discovered the first human coronavirus also investigated bronchitis in... chickens! TRUE/FALSE

Answer: They're ALL true. Thank goodness that June Almeida looked at all those coughing chickens! She was the daughter of a Scottish bus driver and left school at 16, but she'd go on to become a pioneer after getting her first job as a lab technician. She trained herself to be a hot shot with an electron microscope. When she was sent nasal washings from a school, she put them under her microscope and was the first person ever to spot ... the coronavirus!

85

THE SPECKLED MONSTER!

Smallpox affected humans for thousands of years. But in the Middle Ages, the smallpox virus really hit humans. It caused fever and vomiting followed by sores in the mouth and blisters on the skin.

People were so scared of the disease they called it the "Speckled Monster."

Smallpox even plagued Queen Elizabeth I of England. She was ill with what people thought was a cold, that became a fever, that turned out to be ... smallpox.

At first, the queen refused to believe she could catch such a dreadful disease! Queen Elizabeth came near to death and was nursed by her friend, Lady Mary Sidney.

Lady Mary became terribly disfigured and like many women of the time, she took to wearing thick white make-up.

But this monster was around before the Elizabethans. People think it stretches back as far as another royal family...

...the Egyptian Pharaohs! When the mummy of Pharaoh Ramesses V was found by Egyptologists, he was covered in lesions which were probably caused by Smallpox.

DO PLANTS SNEEZE?

Well, they might not sneeze, but they can become ill. Did you know that a virus with no known cure can even infect plants? The first plant virus was detected by scientists in the 19th century, and it was called the Tobacco Mosaic Virus.

Can you guess why? Of course, because it was first discovered on the tobacco plant! This rod-shaped virus also affects tomatoes and peppers. Symptoms included mottling, turning yellow, stunted growth, and crinkled leaves.

ACHOO!

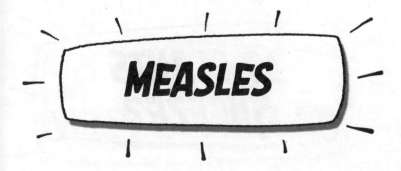

Ever come out in pimples? All over your body? Then you might have had a bout of measles. This highly infectious virus can cause illness for 7-10 days and cause:

Symptoms:

- fever
- cough
- runny nose
- red, inflamed eyes
- rash

can also cause other more serious problem such as:

- seizures
- blindness
- swelling of the brain!

Fortunately, we're able to keep measles under control by using vaccines.

HOW NEWS OF THE FLU FLEW

THE GOOD NEWS: for most people, a bout of influenza ('flu' for short) may not be serious.

THE BAD NEWS: influenza has killed more people than any other virus around the world.

The flu of 1918 was the deadliest worldwide explosion of flu, coinciding with the First World War. It was such a big deal that newspapers carried ads to recruit nurses!

Where did this flu originate? We're not sure exactly!

But it was first reported in Spain—even the king fell ill with it. At the time, other countries also had cases of flu but the war was still going on, which meant that newspapers in places such as Britain, Germany, and France weren't allowed to mention a deadly virus. Why not? The politicians didn't want to lower morale.

Spain was neutral in the war, so it didn't matter so much if cases were reported—and so the flu got its name!

Did You Know?

The 1918 pandemic killed more than 50 million people. Scientists recently set out to reconstruct this virus—and succeeded!

Why did they want to do this? To find out more about how it was so rapidly transferred from one person to another.

At the time, people thought the flu would mean the end of humankind!

HIV AND AIDS

Acquired Immunodeficiency Syndrome or AIDs is a disease that hit pandemic proportions in the early 1980s.

The first infected person was identified in 1959.

Years later, Françoise Barré-Sinoussi and Luc Montagnier took cells from infected patients and later identified the virus which causes AIDS. It became known as the Human Immunodeficiency Virus or HIV.

Immunodeficiency means "lack of an immune system."

This virus attacks the very thing in the body that's there to fight viruses and other types of invader: a person's immune system. It's a type of virus called a "retrovirus"–weakening the immune system until an infected person can no longer fight infections.

The virus spread due to differences in the way people lived.

HIV is spread through some bodily fluids. If these details had been understood sooner, the spread may have been reduced earlier.

Fortunately, there are now antiretroviral treatments available that reduce the amount of HIV virus in a person's body. This means that people with HIV can now live long and healthy lives!

SCIENCE NEVER STOPS-- JUST BECAUSE A SCIENTIST STOPS, THE SCIENCE SHOULD NOT STOP!

Luc Montagnier

Françoise Barré-Sinoussi

TOP TEN TERRIBLES

In the table opposite, we have ten of the most terrible illnesses to affect humankind. Each one of these deadly diseases killed large numbers of people.

But what organism was the culprit behind each one? Was it a...

☼ **Viral villain**

☼ **Baddie bacteria**

or

☼ **Preposterous parasite?**

NAME	ANSWER
The Black Death / Bubonic Plague	Baddie Bacteria
Cholera	Baddie Bacteria
Influenza	Viral Villain
Malaria	Preposterous Parasite
Tuberculosis	Baddie Bacteria
Measles	Viral Villain
Smallpox	Viral Villain
HIV/AIDs	Viral Villain
Ebola	Viral Villain
COVID-19	Viral Villain

THE BIG ONES ...

Which were the two deadliest pandemics ever?

1. The Black Death, 1340s AD

This was the deadliest pandemic in human history, caused by a bacterium called *Yersinia pestis.* It was transmitted by fleas. Poor rats got the blame, but it looks like people's bad hygiene may have been the cause. Up to 25 million people died of the plague.

2. Influenza, 1918

The 1918 Influenza pandemic started in February 1918 and ended in April 1920. It infected a third of the world's population—about 500 million people!

Pandemics caused by viruses are more likely these days. But why?

| **Two reasons ...** |

1. The discovery of penicillin by trailblazing scientist Sir Alexander Fleming in 1928, which makes him a medical superhero! Penicillin works against bacteria, but not viruses.

2. A connected world—more people travel around the world now, meaning viruses are able to spread faster!

The discovery of antibiotics like penicillin means that many bacterial diseases are now treatable, BUT the problem of antibiotic resistance is a MASSIVE issue.

If bacteria become resistant to our antibiotics, meaning they can fight off the drug, we'll see the re-emergence of bacteria-related diseases too.
That's why scientists have to keep on working to find better drugs and better treatments.

Be a Great Plague Doctor!

The Great Plague was a version of the Bubonic Plague that hit 17th-Century London. It was transmitted by rat fleas (ouch!). If you were a Great Plague doctor, what notes would you scribble into a notebook after visiting a patient?

WHAT YOU WORE
It might have been a beak! Plague doctors wore leather beaks stuffed with dried flowers, herbs, and a sponge soaked in vinegar. The theory was that this would protect them from disease. The theory was wrong!

WHAT SYMPTOMS YOU SAW
Fever and chills, infected swellings, vomiting, and weakness—even bleeding from the mouth or rear end!

YOUR QUALIFICATIONS
Many doctors at the time had NO formal training!

WHAT TREATMENTS YOU GAVE
You could prescribe sorrel, dandelion, or sage. Other foodstuffs included brown bread and beer. You might even have created an astrological chart for the patient!

CHAPTER 7

CONQUERING COVID-19

Vaccines have helped turn the tide against COVID–19 ... but there's still lots to do to keep everyone safe.

REDUCING THE RISK

On December 8, 2020, a UK grandmother became the first person in the world to receive an approved vaccine for SARS-CoV-2. The vaccine is life changing and life SAVING. Does that mean we've all done our bit, and can go back to playing Animal Crossing?

NO!

To put the pandemic behind us, once and for all, we need to change the way we live. Particularly as pandemics caused by viruses are more likely these days (see pages 96-97).

What FIVE things can YOU do to make a difference?

Socially distance yourself from people not in your bubble.

Wear a face covering— what design will you have on yours?

Wash your hands, to break down the envelope of the coronavirus!

Cheer up friends and family members by speaking to them on the phone or online.

Raise awareness: share accurate science,

Helping You Help

Dr. Katrine Wallace calls herself a Nerd, but she's also an Epidemiologist—that's a doctor of public health. She shares with the public important facts about how to reduce SARS-CoV-2 transmission. Dr Kat checks infection rates and advises people on how to slow the spread of a virus. **(She also rides a scooter to work! Go Dr Kat!)**

THE VACCINE LADDER

Did you know that after clean water, vaccines have saved more lives than any other intervention? But this doesn't happen overnight. First, the vaccine has to go through lots of stages. It's like climbing the rungs of a ladder to get to the top—or the patient!

Here's what a Vaccine Ladder might look like...

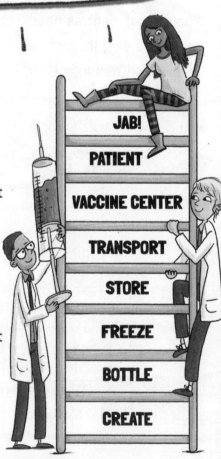

JAB!

PATIENT

VACCINE CENTER

TRANSPORT

STORE

FREEZE

BOTTLE

CREATE

Vaccines need to be stored at the right temperature in order to be safely shipped to hospitals, pharmacists, and doctors' surgeries all around the world. Some of the COVID-19 vaccines are kept at -95°F (-70°C)! That's colder than the ARCTIC.

Vaccination centres need lots of space to deal with people coming through. Look at these unusual places that we never thought would become medical facilities!

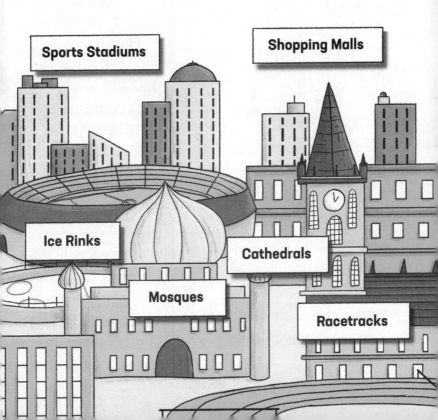

Sports Stadiums

Shopping Malls

Ice Rinks

Cathedrals

Mosques

Racetracks

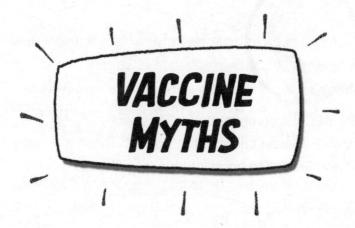

VACCINE MYTHS

Here are some vaccine myths that you can help to **DEBUNK!**

WEREN'T THE COVID-19 VACCINES RUSHED?

NO! The COVID-19 vaccines were developed quickly, that's true. This was down to **funding** (everyone emptied their piggy banks) and the international **science community working together,** plus previous **research into coronaviruses.**

BUT the clinical trials, which look at safety and effect on human beings, weren't rushed at all. **Phew!**

BUT THERE WILL BE LONG-TERM SIDE EFFECTS!

UNLIKELY! A complication or side effect from a vaccine (like an allergic reaction) will usually occur within minutes to hours of receiving the jab.

YOU CAN GET COVID-19 FROM THE VACCINE!

FALSE! There's no live virus in the vaccines, so they can't infect you. You might have side effects like an achey arm where you were vaccinated, or you may have a headache or tiredness, but that's due to your body's immune response. It means the vaccine is working!

I'VE HAD COVID, SO I DON'T NEED A VACCINE!

ARE YOU SURE? Evidence suggests that the vaccine offers better protection than having had the virus. Also, we don't know how long immunity lasts—so having the vaccine means long-term protection. Play it safe and get a jab.

MAKING MONSTERS

A virus can be a Mutating Monster. It changes all the time to infect people.

SARS-CoV-2 is no exception. Thousands of mutations have occurred, changing how deadly it is and how easily it spreads. If that sounds scary, it doesn't need to be. Think of it like a battle. Zombie Mutations versus Humans!

Natural Selection

In 1859, **Charles Darwin** described his theory of evolution by natural selection. He helped to explain why different species exist. He said that if individuals adapt to their environment, they are more likely to survive and reproduce. **This is the same for viruses.**

But does this mean that a Zombie Mutation will win the battle?

NO—HUMANS WIN!

Super scientists continue their work, day and night! Zombie Mutations may reduce the impact of a vaccine, BUT technology is constantly updated.

The new mRNA Vaccines can be modified super quickly! Booster shots are being developed regularly, to help humans win the battle with the mutated virus.

Vaccine Victors

Dr. Anna Blackney and **Dr. Paul McKay** worked on creating an mRNA vaccine at Imperial College London ... but they haven't stopped. Now, they monitor the virus and continue to change the vaccine as the villainous virus changes.

• **They design vaccines, thinking about how they'll work...**

• **...Then they create vaccines inside their labs, working with lots of up-to-date equipment.**

• **They finish the vaccine and send it off to be tested in clinical trials - ready to fight new mutant viruses!**

VANQUISHING CORONAVIRUS

Smallpox first appeared 3,000 years ago. It was vanquished in 1980. Even today, Smallpox remains the only virus that has ever been fully erased.

Just like Smallpox, COVID-19 will not be quick to vanquish. But we can limit its spread. What will that take? These are questions still to answer...

Will COVID-19...
- ☼ Come in a set of waves, like flu?
- ☼ Hang about as a determined disease, always there?
- ☼ Disappear completely?

Most experts believe the answers to the first two questions are **YES**. **Here's why...**

The virus has spread to lots of communities. This makes it difficult to get rid of once and for all. This situation is described as 'endemic' - always around.

COVID-19 is likely to return in seasonal waves or small outbreaks. But don't worry. We have vaccines! We will be able to contain outbreaks in the future.

Moving On

What happens next depends on **FIVE** important questions. The answers will help us cure the world.

✪ **HOW** will we work together to send vaccines to the countries who need them?

✪ **WHAT** will we do to educate each other?

✪ **WHERE** does the virus enter the body?

✪ **WHEN** will normal life resume?

✪ **WHICH** new medicines will we collaborate on to help treat COVID-19?

STAYING TOGETHER

Many people around the world have died due to coronavirus and others have long-term health problems due to their infection. This is no one's fault, and it's alright to feel worried sometimes.

The world has been a scary place.

It's OK to be unsure. It's OK to be scared. And it's definitely OK to offer, give, or ask for help. We should talk about our thoughts and feelings regularly with our loved ones, and teachers. The more we talk about difficult situations, the better we will feel. Here's how you can help your parents, siblings, friends ... and how to help yourself.

TOP TEN TOGETHER TIPS

1.	Keep a routine	**6**	Stick to the facts
2.	Ask for a hug	**7.**	Try calming craft activities
3.	Share a story	**8.**	Draw pictures
4.	Don't hide your worries	**9.**	Be patient
5.	Ask how you can help	**10.**	Show love

These important skills will last a lifetime and help build memories for the people lost.

Thank You Key Workers!

Key workers are superheroes! They have helped us get through so many difficult times. Why don't you design a superhero costume for a key worker you know? What would it look like and why? What tools or protection would they have? Use paint or pencils to keep it bright and beautiful!

KEY WORKERS INCLUDE:

Teachers

Postal Workers

Doctor and nurses

Supermarket workers

Caretakers

CHAPTER 8

THE FUTURE, A NEW WORLD

This coronavirus is here for the long haul — here's what scientists predict for the next months and years.

SAY HI TO TECH!

During the pandemic, people could only go to the doctors for an emergency. This meant that something called telemedicine became the new normal. Telemedicine is the act of caring for patients remotely. Have you had a doctor's appointment online or over the phone?

Wearing Your Medicine
New, wearable devices such as fitness trackers are in development to check people's vital signs. Here are just some of the health issues they could track:

- ☼ **Glucose levels for diabetes**
- ☼ **Heart rhythms**
- ☼ **Asthma attacks**
- ☼ **Early detections of illness**

Heart rhythms are monitored by wearing a vest!

Vest with built-in heart monitoring system

Robots, Robots, Everywhere

Some scientists are convinced we'll have a robot revolution as a result of COVID-19. Here are just some of the incredible ways that robots helped during the pandemic. Can you guess which one is NOT true?

- ☼ **Disinfection robots cleaned hospitals in China using ultraviolet light**

- ☼ **Akira the Articulated Arm fed people grapes at their bedside**

- ☼ **Quadcopter drones ferried samples to laboratories**

- ☼ **Tommy the robot nurse monitored patients in Italy**

FALSE: Akira doesn't exist, though we might want her to!

THE GENIUS VACCINE

mRNA vaccines were developed to help conquer COVID-19. But they're not just any vaccine.

IT'S A VERY UNIQUE WAY OF MAKING A VACCINE.

Professor Bekeredjian-Ding, Head of Microbiology, Paul-Ehrlich-Institut, Germany

Why is using mRNA so fascinating?

It helps the body to produce one of the same proteins that's on the virus!

By creating a viral protein—the spike protein on the outside—the body's immune system recognizes them as baddies and attacks them.

The body can now recognize the virus.

This exciting new vaccine could also be developed to treat HIV or certain types of cancer.

'Parton' With Her Dollars

Dolly Parton is a famous American singer who uses her money to spread acts of human benefit. When COVID-19 hit the world, she wanted to help make her fellow human beings better. So she donated money to a hospital that was one of the first to test one of the mRNA vaccines.

Y'ALL NEED TO GET YOUR VACCINES, Y'HEAR?

Dolly Parton

Dolly Parton used her money to help others, but you can volunteer for charities, spread knowledge, shop for others, or help with food banks.

LEARNING FROM EXPERIENCE

The spread of COVID-19 has taught us some important lessons. In the future, we'll be better prepared. We now understand the impact pandemics can have on our health and society.

The next pandemic could be years, decades, or even a century away—but as a species, we'll have lots of knowledge and learning behind us.

We could:

✿ **Use new "mega testing" diagnostic platforms—** this is testing on a mass scale. We could check whole populations for a virus at once, tracing the disease and isolating cases. This would help to stop the spread.

⚙ **Analyze viral genomes faster using AI.** This means we'll also create vaccines faster, too. Plus, we'll understand which treatments will work the best. This means we could protect more people early on.

⚙ **What's bigger than a single brain? An epi-brain!** This is an idea that the World Health Organization has had to help experts combine their public health data to prepare for another emergency. As the Boy Scouts say ... **Be Prepared!**

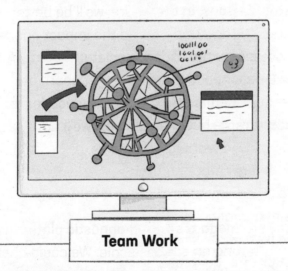

Team Work

We've seen how effective single vaccines can be. But what about a combined approach? Computer modelling makes it possible to use different types of vaccine together, for even better immunity!

MABS, LABS AND LLAMAS!

The body produces antibodies to fight off a virus. Monoclonal antibodies, or mAbs for short, are laboratory-made versions—meaning they're made by scientists, rather than by your own body!

Antibodies, whether natural (made by our immune system) or monoclonal (made by a super scientist), can stick directly to a virus, trapping it inside an antibody prison, and stopping it from infecting cells.

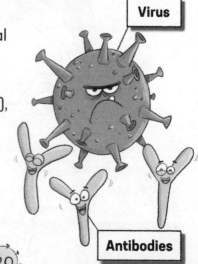

Virus

Antibodies

Lab-made monoclonal antibodies have also been shown to provide short-term protection from SARS-CoV-2, and could serve as another important tool in our ever-growing toolbox against COVID-19.

And if that's not enough ... **WE HAVE LLAMAS TOO**.

LLAMAS? Yes.

Scientists have recently discovered that llamas have another type of protein called "nanobodies"—similar to antibodies—that have been shown to be effective against COVID-19. Cormac, a llama at a farm in the US, helped with this incredible research!

A DEADLY DISCOVERY?

We've learned a lot about our health and about how to prevent the next pandemic. But we still have a LOT to learn about the incredible world of viruses.

 **READER'S VOICE**

BUT I'VE JUST READ THIS ENTIRE BOOK! HOW CAN THERE BE MORE?

It's likely that there are millions of viruses still waiting to be discovered.

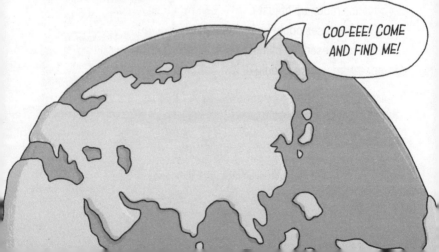

COO-EEE! COME AND FIND ME!

The Frosty Virus...

Recently, a new source of viruses emerged. Well, not so new. It's actually 30,000 years old! But it was first discovered in 2015. Researchers found an ancient virus called *Pithovirus sibericum*. It had been dormant for centuries, frozen in a deep layer of the Siberian permafrost. But after it thawed, it became infectious again.

...the Big Thaw

Luckily for the scientists and their pack of intrepid huskies* who stumbled across it, there was no risk to humans or animals this time! This virus infects amoebas, which are organisms made up of just one cell. But there is a real risk that other viruses could be unleashed as more ground becomes exposed. As climate change increases the world's temperatures, more deadly diseases could emerge.

*Okay, we don't know if they actually had a pack of huskies!

A NEW WORLD

With tantalizing tech, and changes to the way we live—the world will be a different place after COVID-19.

Cities will change: The pandemic taught us that people no longer always need to commute to an office. They can work remotely. Families may move out of cities to rural areas, changing communities in many different ways!

Human interactions: Lockdowns made us all realize how important connection really is. People NEED to connect in person, so community groups and social events will only increase. Who wants to start an online science club?

Virology: More research into SARS-CoV-2 will allow doctors and scientists to further understand how viruses cause disease, and how we can prevent them. But we should remember that not all viruses are bad. Some viruses that live in the human body may keep us healthy, and others are essential for keeping ecosystems running smoothly by helping to recycle essential nutrients. Humans wouldn't be able to survive without them.

Planet Earth: The way the pandemic has affected us all made us realize that we need to take care of ourselves and our planet. With people moving away from cities, will we take more care of the environment? We also have other challenges to deal with—like the plastic pollution in our oceans and the climate emergency.

Can we collaborate and work on these scientific conundrums together too?

WE SURE CAN.

And we'll need you—our **FUTURE LEADERS**, **SCIENTISTS**, **DOCTORS**, **NURSES**, **RESEARCHERS**, and **SUPERHEROES** ...
... to help make our **DREAMS** become our **FUTURE**.
A NEW WORLD.

Remember, if viruses can adapt and change—so can we. **And we will.**

Create your own Time Capsule

COVID-19 will go down in history as a time of great change. So people have been encouraged to keep diaries, blogs, photo records, and share daily thoughts. This will help future historians understand what the world was like during a pandemic!

YOU COULD HELP! HERE'S HOW:

1. Find a capsule. This could be an empty candy tin or shoe box.

2. Fill the capsule with objects that represent your daily life. Make sure that you don't take anything without permission. These could include a handprint, family photo, comics, craft supplies...

3. Write a note to include in the time capsule. You could talk about who you are and what you like doing each day.

4. SEAL your capsule!

Choose a safe place to store your time capsule. This could be the back of a cupboard, or you could even bury it in your yard!

Imagine who might discover your gift to the world in hundreds of years' time ... from the time when we vanquished a virus.

Now you know how to VANQUISH A VIRUS!